WATER, WATER EVERYWHERE!
STOP POLLUTION, SAVE OUR OCEANS
CONSERVATION FOR KIDS

Children's Conservation Books

pfiffikus

EDUCATIONAL BOOKS FOR CHILDREN K-12

WHAT IS WATER POLLUTION? WHAT ARE ITS CAUSES AND EFFECTS?

HOW SERIOUS IS WATER POLLUTION?

The most important element on Earth is water. All living things need it. But it's depressing to note that safe drinking water is becoming less available. It's because of pollution.

We should prevent water pollutants getting into the water. Household wastes should be disposed of properly. Lawn fertilizers should be managed properly.

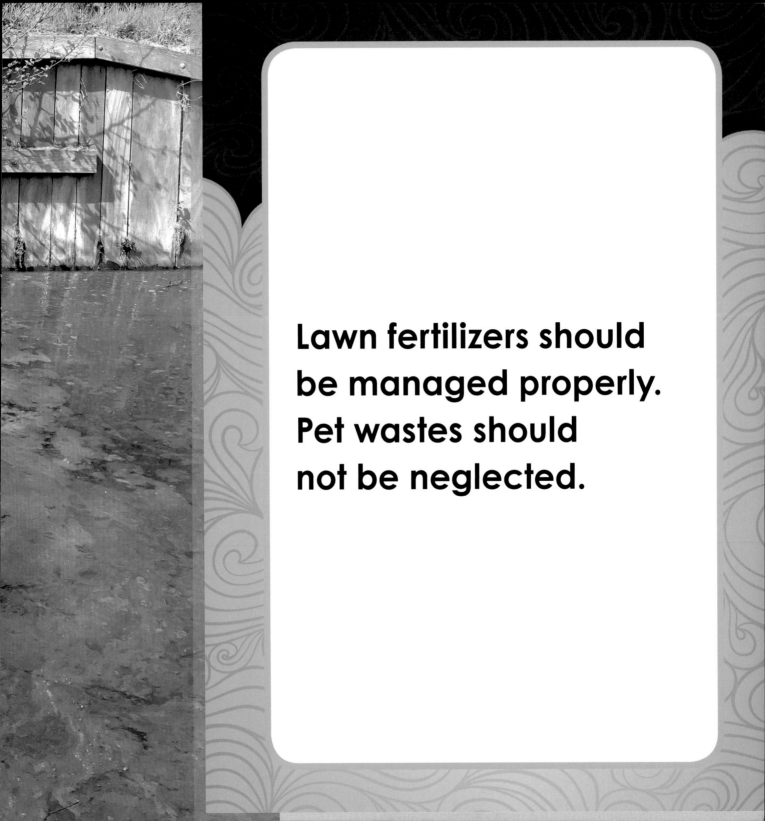

Lawn fertilizers should
be managed properly.
Pet wastes should
not be neglected.

All these contaminants can cause a critical condition in bodies of water or the whole water table.
If the water is contaminated, it is not fit for use.

A small quantity of these toxic substances may bring less harm. But we have to accept the fact that the Earth has increased its population over the years, and that every person creates waste.

WHAT DO YOU THINK WILL HAPPEN?

Water pollution brings damage to the rivers, lakes, oceans and other water sources.

Our clean water resources are not dumping sites! They have to be protected from pollution.

Water pollution is second to air pollution as an environmental concern.

We know that water covers over 2/3 of the Earth's surface. But most of that water is salt, not fresh. As the population continues to grow, our water resources come under pressure from human activities.

The water's quality is reduced. People tend to misuse water resources. Water pollution is one of the biggest problems that Earth is facing.

Water pollution means
poor water quality.
Due to recent developments
spread out on Earth,
human problems occur.

These problems pose a serious threat to the Earth. People used to think that oceans would not be affected by human abuse.

They thought that the ocean was just too big to pollute. But people have exceeded with even what the oceans can absorb.

Toxic materials that humans create result in pollution. It is a threat to life. It's a threat to the Earth!

All water resources including the oceans are contaminated. Let's stop water pollution now! Let's save the Earth before it disappears to oblivion.

WHAT IS WATER POLLUTION?

ARE WE EXPERIENCING ITS EFFECTS?

It simply means that substances are added into the water which makes it dangerous for animals and people to use.

These toxic substances will have an effect on the water's quality. This could harm lives that depend on the water.

These include humans, plants and animals. Pollutants like chemicals are disposed directly or indirectly into the water sources without giving them enough treatment.

These chemicals modify the properties of the water, making it detrimental to living things.

Water pollution is
mainly caused by
human acts.
Water pollution comes
in different types.

NUTRIENT POLLUTION

This is done by fertilizers and sewage in water bodies.

High nutrient levels encourage the growth of algae which can make water undrinkable. They can clog filters.

SURFACE WATER POLLUTION

These involve bodies of water on the Earth's surface, like rivers and oceans. When hazardous chemicals get into the water's surface, it can cause pollution.

GROUND WATER POLLUTION

This is caused by pesticides and chemicals we apply on the soil. These can cause underground water pollution as these chemicals get washed deep into the ground by rain water.

Let us increase the amount of safe water. With your own little ways, you can help save water from being polluted. Simply doing proper waste management is already a big help!

71826250R00024

Made in the USA
Lexington, KY
24 November 2017